995

D1060161

HERITAGE HOUSES

The American Tradition in Connecticut 1660-1900

Sara Emerson Rolleston

Foreword by David W. Dangremond

A Studio Book
The Viking Press
New York

For my beloved husband, William Anthony Rolleston, A.I.A.,
whose helping hand made this book possible.

Copyright © Sara Emerson Rolleston 1979

All rights reserved

First published in 1979 by The Viking Press/A Studio Book
625 Madison Avenue, New York, N.Y. 10022

Published simultaneously in Canada by
Penguin Books Canada Limited

Library of Congress Cataloging in Publication Data
Rolleston, Sara Emerson.
Heritage houses.
(A Studio book)
1. Historic buildings—Connecticut—Guide-books.
2. Connecticut—History, Local.   3. Architecture,
Domestic—Connecticut.   I. Title.
F95.R64   974.6   79-14854
ISBN 0-670-36880-6

Printed in the United States of America by
The Murray Printing Company,
Westford, Massachusetts
Set in Baskerville
Designed by Michael Shroyer

Acknowledgments

I am much indebted to the many historical societies and individuals who opened their doors to me, allowing me to intrude into their lives for whole days to photograph this chronicle of Connecticut's domestic architecture. This book, through the cooperation of many, is another way to preserve the record of the important artistic achievements of the past.

Special thanks must go first of all to my husband, William A. Rolleston, A.I.A., whose interest and cooperation in this project have been constant.

To David W. Dangremond, administrator of the Webb-Deane-Stevens museum houses, I express my thanks for the Foreword, and for the wonderful freedom he and the Society of the Colonial Dames of America gave me to photograph the three houses. I also appreciate the assistance of Mrs. Gary V. Weigel.

Heartfelt gratitude is offered to the following people, who so generously, in one way or another, furthered this project: Mr. Dory Alvers, Mr. Ford Ballard, Mrs. Mary Barlow, Mr. Richard Bennett and the Hartford National Bank and Trust Company, Mr. William Bilbert, Mr. and Mrs. John Blum, Mrs. Ludlow Bull, Mr. George Campbell, Mrs. Maynard Campbell, Mr. and Mrs. William Sheffield Cowles, the Connecticut Daughters of the American Revolution, Mrs. Milo Dotson, Mr. and Mrs. Albert Faust, Mr. Wilson H. Faude, Mrs. H. Sage Goodwin, Miss Helen Green, Mrs. Mary Griswold, Mr. Robert Gunshanon, Miss Evelyn Hamlin, Mrs. Lynn Hanson, Mrs. Thomas Hart, Mr. John Haynes, Mrs. Janet Jainschigg, Mr. Philip Johnson, Mrs. Frederick Kunkel, Mr. and Mrs. Ralph C. Lasbury, and Mr. Arthur Leibundguth.

Also, Mr. Charles Miller, Mrs. A. Gibbs Mitchell, Master Kenneth Moran, Mrs. Manley Moran, Mrs. Robert Montgomery, Miss Margaret McIntyre, the National Society of the Colonial Dames in Connecticut, Mrs. Robert Nicoll, Miss Evelyn Phelps, Mrs. Newell Pinkham, Mrs. David Pinsky, Mrs. Robert Pittaway, Mrs. Janice C. Reimer, Mrs. Frank Roethel, Mrs. Ruth Rouse, Mrs. Henry R. Rousseau, Mrs. Theodore Rudd, Mrs. Harlow Savage, Miss Ellice A. Scofield, Mrs. Stuart Segar, Mr. Jack Shannahan, Mrs. Godfrey Shaw, Mr. Robert Silliman, Mrs. Howard Simpson, Mrs. Robert Spellman, Mr. and Mrs. John H. Spencer, Mrs. Elaine Stetson, Mr. Ellsworth Stoughton, Mr. Jarold Talbot, Mr. James B. Tanner, Mr. and Mrs. Russel Taylor, Mr. James McA. Thompson, Miss Barbara Todd, Mr. William Van Bynan, Mr. Joseph S. Van Why, Miss Frances Wells, Mr. and Mrs. Winthrop Wilson, Mr. and Mrs. Richard Wolf, Dr. and Mrs. James H. Wright, and Dr. and Mrs. Constantine Zariphes.

To Mary Velthoven, Michael Shroyer, and Stephen Sechrist of Studio Books go my special thanks for their talented efforts in helping to develop this book.

Contents

Foreword

Connecticut, although it is the third smallest state in the nation, has one of the country's richest and most diverse architectural histories. Here the rough-hewn timbers of a seventeenth-century dwelling stand in sharp contrast to the sleek geometry of a glass house by Philip Johnson. Here, within a few miles, are narrow streets lined with ship captains' houses, stretches of green bordered by merchants' mansions, and picturesque hillsides dotted with neat clapboard dwellings behind solid stone walls. Here too are the academic buildings at Yale, the gleaming corporate headquarters in Stamford, and the many-towered cityscape of Hartford. Worthy representatives of four centuries of Connecticut architecture stand side by side in pleasing visual harmony.

The remarkable survival of Connecticut's early architecture is no accident. The history of preservation in the state is a long and distinguished one. The Colonial Dames and the Antiquarian and Landmarks Society were among the first groups in the state to restore and furnish historic houses and open them to the public. The advice and craftsmanship of architectural experts like Norman Isham, J. Frederick Kelly, and Frédéric Palmer assured the accuracy of these early restorations. Today, more than five hundred historic houses in the state are open to the public on a regular basis. Countless others have been privately restored and continue life as dwellings or, after sympathetic adaptation, find new life through other uses. This balance of public and private preservation efforts, so vital to the continuing preservation of Connecticut buildings, is an important feature of this new book by Sara Emerson Rolleston.

The handsome photographs present a sampler of three centuries of Connecticut houses. Focusing on the eighteenth century, the richest period in Connecticut's architectural history, Mrs. Rolleston has captured the rugged house frames of the early Connecticut builders, the highly original creations of Connecticut cabinetmakers, and the skillfully wrought productions of Connecticut craftsmen with great sensitivity and skill. The armchair visitor is provided with an informative and relaxing tour of some of the finest Connecticut houses, many never before seen by the public. One cannot turn the pages of this book without gaining a knowledge of the rich cultural heritage of Connecticut and a vivid glimpse of a world many of us have left behind.

David W. Dangremond
Administrator
The Webb–Deane–Stevens Museum

Introduction

One July day when I was photographing one of the historic houses pictured in this book (a seventeenth-century structure with great wide fireplaces and heavily beamed ceilings) a family of visitors arrived. Father, mother, and two teen-age children, they had traveled all the way from Texas to explore what they called "their American heritage." The houses they had searched out to visit in this tiny state, they said, belonged to every American citizen, to Californians and Texans, to residents of Colorado and Maine, just as much as to residents of Connecticut. Many of the deep roots of American life were established in houses such as the one this family was visiting.

As I went about focusing my camera and lighting my room scenes, I felt an empathy with these travelers, for their visit expressed just what I was trying to say with my camera. During the months in which I had been going from house to house taking pictures, I had become deeply impressed by the extent to which Connecticut's legacy of magnificent architecture does belong to all Americans, in much the same way that Plymouth Plantation or Sturbridge Village in Massachusetts, Shelburne in Vermont, and Williamsburg in Virginia do. Here in these houses early pioneers lived and broke the back of the wilderness. They built their homes here and raised children who in time became leaders helping to fulfill the American dream. Jonathan Trumbull, Oliver Ellsworth, and Noah Webster were products of this environment. Great merchants such as Ebenezer Grant, Joseph Webb, and Samuel Russell, and writers like Harriet Beecher Stowe and Mark Twain, lived in the Connecticut River Valley. The houses of farmers, blacksmiths, and leather workers are also shown in this book, for they too played an important part in the unfolding of American history.

In the framework of the early houses we can see how the posts and plates, the summer beams and joists, the girts and rafters were put together by methods that were common throughout New England. Many were really earth ships built by shipbuilders. Their rugged skeletons secured by mortise-and-tenon joints, these sturdy structures have weathered the storms of centuries.

In this day of microwave ovens, gas and electric ranges, an encounter with a Colonial kitchen is a stern reminder that all seventeenth-century baking and cooking was done over an open hearth fire. Looms and spinning wheels reaffirm that all thread and yarns had to be spun by hand from flax, hemp, cotton, or wool after long preparation of the fiber, then handwoven into fabric. Bed linens, coverlets, blankets, and materials for clothing, curtains, table and pillow covers, and simple upholstery were woven at home, although some of the finer fabrics were imported from abroad. At first animal pelts were used for rugs; later there were hooked, braided, and woven rag rugs. Oriental rugs were imported by the well-to-do, and often were used as table covers. Candles, reeds, or "betty lamps" were the materials for illumination before oil lamps were used. Mattresses were stuffed with corn husks or feathers, and feather beds were warmed with warming pans filled with hot coals to relieve the penetrating chill of houses that knew no central heating. Many of the houses in this book are still furnished (or have been refurnished) with the chairs, beds, tables, cabinets, and household implements that belonged to their early owners. A step across the threshold is a step into history and the way of life of the original inhabitants.

The coming to these shores of the Pilgrims in 1620 and the founding of Plymouth Plantation, the arrival of the Puritans in 1630 under the charter of the Massachusetts Bay Company, and the establishment of Salem, Boston, Charlestown, Medford, Weymouth, Roxbury, Ipswich, Watertown, Lynn, Dorchester, and Newtown (now Cambridge) were all accomplished in a period of about fourteen years. Within that short span of time, the expansion into Connecticut had already begun.

Many factors motivated the shiploads of people who came to New England year after year, but a primary one was the desire to worship in their own way and evade the persecutions and imprisonments inflicted upon them in England. The Pilgrims and Puritans took the Bible literally. Identifying themselves with the children of Israel, they too went into a wilderness searching for an escape from tyranny and the promised land. The overwhelming desire to practice their own beliefs spurred a willingness to suffer the hardships of the long voyage and the dangers of the wilderness.

The history of Plymouth, the Massachusetts Bay Company, and the early Connecticut settlements is replete with the names of people who, had they stayed in England, might have led equally significant lives. William Bradford, Myles Standish, John Alden, John Winthrop, Thomas Hooker, and John Davenport were towering figures of their day.

One of the first prominent figures in Connecticut history was John Oldham, who came to this country in 1623 and settled in Watertown, Massachusetts. In 1630, he became a "free-man," recognized as a man of substance and entitled to a vote in community affairs. Both William Bradford and John Winthrop described him as a bit of a bounder and troublemaker, but he was respected as a trader and explorer. In 1633, he journeyed overland to the Connecticut River. Members of the Plymouth colony already had a trading post operating in competition with one established earlier by Dutch traders from New Amsterdam near what is now Windsor. Oldham explored the Connecticut River Valley and brought back to Watertown samples of hemp, luxurious pelts, and enthusiastic tales of "many very desirable places upon the same river, fit to receive many hundred inhabitants." In 1634, a group from Watertown set forth and erected a few huts at what is now Wethersfield, enduring a hard and difficult winter. In 1635, others from Watertown joined that group. The following year most of the congregation of the First Church of Christ of Newtown left Massachusetts en masse under the leadership of their preacher, Thomas Hooker (1586–1647) and Samuel Stone, to build the settlement of Hartford, naming it for the town in England where Stone was born.

Cotton Mather, in his essay on Thomas Hooker in Book III of *Magnalia Christi Americana,* tells that "in the Month of June 1636, they removed an Hundred Miles to the Westward, with a purpose to settle upon the delightful Banks of Connecticut River: And there were about an Hundred

Persons in the first Company that made this Removal; who not being able to walk above Ten Miles a Day, took up near a Fortnight in the Journey. . . ." John Winthrop records the event: "Mr. Hooker, pastor of the church of Newtown and the most of his congregation, went to Connecticut. His wife was carried in a horse litter; and they drove one hundred and sixty cattle, and fed of their milk by the way."

The Dorchester church, under the pastor John Warham, removed from thence to establish Windsor in the summer of 1635. Wethersfield, Hartford, and Windsor were in close proximity to each other and by the end of 1636 there were "about two hundred and fifty men in the three towns on the river, and there were twenty men in the garrison, at the entrance of it, under the command of lieutenant Gardiner. The whole consisted, probably, of about eight hundred persons, or of a hundred and sixty or seventy families," as Benjamin Trumbull wrote in *A Complete History of Connecticut, Civil and Ecclesiastical, from the Immigration of Its First Planters from England, in The Year 1630 to the Year 1764,* published in 1818. The garrison to which he refers was a fort near Lyme and Saybrook established by John Winthrop Jr., son of the governor of Massachusetts.

The new settlers began building right away. In the lands along the "Quonehtacut," or Connecticut, they had found their promised land, their Canaan. The landscape was breathtaking. Huge trees, mighty as the cedars of Lebanon, yielded sturdy timbers from which they would carve their "mansion-houses." Fertile fields held the promise of a rich harvest, and, as the seasons progressed, the earth did indeed yield her increase, for great crops were traded with the South and West Indies. Berries and nuts were plentiful and the apple orchards year by year became so prodigious that the fruit was not only made into "aplepye" but pressed to produce barrel upon barrel of "cyder." The slow-moving currents of the river supported great schools of fish, especially salmon; and in its tidal reaches oysters, clams, and lobsters were plentiful. The forests teemed with game, food for the table, and wealth for the trapper, for there was a ready market in Europe for the furs of the abundant mink, beavers, racoons, and black, gray, and red fox.

The colonists averaged only about five feet two inches in stature, but their strength was as much in their convictions as in brawn and muscle. As William Bradford wrote in his journal, "The Lord upheld them and had beforehand prepared them," and they accepted the challenges of the new country. They quickly learned to wield an axe and fell a tree, to farm the land, to build a house and make furniture, although some was brought from England. The task of establishing a new community was complicated by the fact that everything had to be done by hand. Planks were sawed by two men, one working below the log in a saw pit. Clapboards were "rived" or split by hand with axes and wedges. Timbers for the house were cut and framed on the ground beforehand, so that on "raising day" all hands might cooperate in securing the framework to the foundation before the sun had set. Despite the difficulties, the colonists did not build shacks, as later Western pioneers did; they built quality houses from the outset. Though initially manually unskilled, these English intellectuals and aristocrats met the challenge nobly.

The early settlers seemed to have an uncanny endurance. Benjamin Trumbull, in his *History of Connecticut,* says of Hooker's Hartford group: "This adventure was the more remarkable, as many of this company were persons of figure, who had lived, in England, in honor, affluence, and delicacy, and were entire strangers to fatigue and danger." And danger there was. Though some of the Indians were friendly, others, such as the Pequots, disturbed by the rapid expansion of the settlements, were hostile. On July 20, 1636, John Oldham was murdered by Indians who boarded his pinnace off Block Island, and this and other incidents precipitated the series of confrontations in New England that became known as the Pequot Wars. On April 23, 1637, as a field was being prepared for sowing in Wethersfield, about two hundred Pequots attacked the workers, killing six men and twenty cattle, then went on to kill another man and three women, and finally carried away two young girls. In retaliation a force of forty-two men from Hartford, thirty from Windsor and eighteen from Wethersfield, led by Captain John Mason and Lieutenant Robert Seeley, set forth on an expedition against the Pequots, with the help of some friendly Narragansetts and Mohegans. They took the Pequot camp on the Mystic River by surprise, burned it to the ground, and in fierce hand-to-hand frays annihilated most of the inhabitants.

Though this relieved the settlers' tension somewhat, it was by no means the end of their trouble with Indians. They continued to build fort-like houses with small, high windows and strong batten doors that could be barred with heavy beams at night. Although they gradually acquired touches of elegance and comfort, New England houses remained strongholds until well after King Philip's War (1675–1676) and the French and Indian Wars (1689–1763) had ended.

Connecticut was growing in spite of the dangers. The Connecticut colony, which began with the settlement of Hartford, Windsor, and Wethersfield in 1634 and 1635, had by 1646 expanded to include Fairfield, South Hampton, Farmington, and other towns as well.

Near the mouth of the Connecticut River another Puritan colony was established in 1635, sponsored by an English company headed by William Fienne, Lord Say and Sele (1582–1662), and Robert Greville, Lord Brooke (1608–1643), and named Saybrook in their honor. The next major development was the New Haven colony, started in 1638 by John Davenport (1597–1670) and Theophilus Eaton (1590–1658) and settled by Puritans who had arrived only the year before in Boston.

The communities centered around Hartford adhered to the "Fundamental Orders of Connecticut," rules of conduct adopted in 1639 that were somewhat more liberal than those of Massachusetts. The New Haven group had adopted its own much stricter "Plantation Covenant," firmly based upon Scripture. The two were eventually united under a royal charter that had been secured by the Hartford group in 1662 and was finally accepted by the New Haven colony in 1665. Relatively liberal in its provisions, the charter gave Connecticut a degree of independence that encouraged self-reliant colonial government. The freedom it allowed was threatened when Sir Edmund Andros (1637–1714), the British governor of New York and New England, arrived in Hartford on October 31, 1687, with the intention of seizing the charter. It is said that the colonists purposely dragged out the discussions until after dark. Then, when the lights were suddenly extinguished, the charter was whisked away by Captain Joseph Wadsworth, who hid it in the famed Charter Oak, which stood for many years in Hartford. Andros dissolved the government anyway, but the charter was reinstituted in 1689, after the repressive reign of James II had ended. When Connecticut became a state in 1776, the charter was adopted as the Constitution of Connecticut.

The spirit of the charter and the needs of a pioneering life had a lasting effect on the attitudes of Connecticut citizens. They held dear their rights as individuals, but adhered to a bond that led them to help one another build their houses, watch over their sick, build their church, and worship together at its long services. They depended on one another for safety and friendship, and this bond is represented in the frequent use of the heart in the decoration of their household furnishings.

The society that emerged from these beginnings was strong and valiant primarily because of its moral values. A free democracy could only have arisen out of the principles observed by the settlers—respect for the importance of the individual, personal rectitude, love of right and justice. The church was the center of life, and no town could be incorporated until it had organized and built its house of worship. Architectural triumphs, the churches were the most beautiful buildings in the towns and villages. The bells housed beneath their spires rang not only on Sundays; they proclaimed the evening curfew and any news of importance, and were the signal to gather on the green whenever events of moment occurred. War with the Indians was a constant threat, and the village green was the place where the men of the town met to drill and practice marksmanship on "traynin days." And when the training was done, all the town came out to share in the cider and gingerbread.

The practical needs of this pioneer society are reflected in the strength and simplicity of the domestic architecture of the early years of Connecticut. Although houses became more elaborate in their decorative details during the eighteenth century, the integrity of design that had characterized the structures of the pioneer builders was retained. It was not until well into the nineteenth century that Connecticut builders, following the Victorian trend, began to employ romantic fantasy in architectural design.

The old houses of Connecticut are bold artistic statements that represent a spirit of freedom and individuality that continues to inspire American architecture. Their artistry and craftsmanship and the values they signify are a heritage that now demands concerted efforts for preservation. For the great houses of the past are fast disappearing, with only the devoted work of a few dedicated organizations and individuals standing between them and extinction. This book is a tribute to their efforts as well as to the houses themselves and the people who built and lived in them.

This symbol at the end of a description indicates that the house is open to the public.

Stanley-Whitman House

c. 1660, Farmington

John Stanley (1624–1706) built this noble oak clapboard house about 1660. The framed overhang of the second floor and the bulbous drop pendants that ornament it are typical of early New England houses, as are the small-paned lead-glass windows positioned high above ground level.

Two large ground-floor rooms, each about fifteen by twenty feet, with two chambers above, form the original architectural plan. A great central chimney between the rooms draws the smoke from all the fireplaces on both floors. A small front-entrance passageway has a turning, tight-fitting staircase that hugs the chimney wall. The centrally positioned front door is directly opposite the stairs. This general plan has become known as the "two-over-two Connecticut Plan" of construction. In 1760, a lean-to kitchen with adjacent buttery and borning rooms at either side was added at the rear of the house, giving it the familiar saltbox profile. Many seventeenth-century New England houses were built and enlarged according to this plan.

Over the centuries, five families lived in the house. Its last private owners, Mr. and Mrs. D. Newton Barney, engaged architect J. Frederick Kelly to restore the house to its original state before it was given, with the surrounding grounds, to the Village Green and Library Association in 1935. With the help of gifts from local residents, the house has been refurnished with seventeenth- and eighteenth-century antiques and in 1961 it was declared a National Historic Landmark.

Above: Hand-wrought iron food turner.

Above right: Burning coals were put in the oven at the rear of the "hall" chimney until it reached baking temperature; the stones retained enough heat to do the cooking.

16

Left: The parlor has an unpainted wooden dado and paneled fireplace wall. An oak summer beam crosses the center of the ceiling. A Williams Orton Preston clock made in Farmington about 1830 rests on a carved Hadley chest.

Above: The "hall chamber" (the room above the hall) houses spinning, carding, and weaving equipment as well as several small beds.

Right: This ingenious lighting device may hold a candle or, in extremity, a dried reed.

Page 15: The "hall" or kitchen was where Colonial families did most of their living as well as cooking and eating. Tables often were collapsible so they could be stored when not in use. Herbs and spices were stored in the drawers of the wall box at left.

17

Leffingwell Inn

1675, Norwich

The town of Norwich began as an English settlement in 1659, when the Mohegan leader, Uncas, sold a nine-mile-square tract of land to some colonists from Saybrook. In 1675, Stephen Backus built a house there, which he sold to Ensign Thomas Leffingwell in 1700. The new owner was granted permission in 1701 to keep a "publique house of entertainment for strangers," and in 1715 he considerably enlarged the original building. The ownership passed to Thomas's son Benajah in 1724, who left it to his son, Colonel Christopher Leffingwell in 1756.

Christopher Leffingwell was a businessman who inaugurated many enterprises, including a stocking factory and the first papermill in Connecticut. He also owned a pottery workshop, a fulling mill, a chocolate mill, a clothier's shop, and a dye house. About 1760, he too made structural changes in the house's structure. In the tavern room, which had formed the eighteen-by-twenty-foot first floor of Stephen Backus's dwelling, he added paneling that was furred out a foot from the original walls all around the room, reducing the room's dimensions to sixteen by eighteen feet. New cupboards were installed,

and in the backs of the cupboards the original 1675 paneling can be found.

The building was scheduled for demolition by the state highway department in 1956, but through the efforts of the noted antiquarian Elmer D. Keith it was turned over to The Society of the Founders of Norwich Connecticut, Inc., instead. The inn was then moved to its present site on Washington Street and completely restored and refurnished. During the restoration, fragments from the original diamond-paned leaded windows were found in the recess between the paneling and the outer walls.

The Leffingwell Inn was a gathering place for patriots during the Revolutionary War. On April 8, 1776, George Washington visited Christopher Leffingwell here to seek his aid in the war effort and they breakfasted together in the north parlor.

Viewed from the front, Leffingwell Inn looks like a simple square two-story house, but it is actually composed of two saltbox sections set together at right angles. At the rear, the angle of the roof falls away in a long trough to form a single story.

Right: A brass kettle rests on an English pierced brass trivet.

Opposite left: Christopher Leffingwell's third wife, Ruth Perit Leffingwell.

Left: A hand-carved wooden doll wears her original cape, bonnet, and indigo blue dress.

Below: The tavern room of Leffingwell Inn.

Page 19: The chamber over the tavern room, with its two great summer beams, is largely as it was in 1675.

Sergeant Deming House

1666, Hartford County

The red-plank saltbox built in 1666 for Sergeant John Deming has been owned through the years by direct descendants or relatives of his family. Originally it was a typical two-over-two Connecticut Plan house. A lean-to kitchen was added later. In 1847, the Deming family sold the house to a relative, Winthrop Buck, who used it as living quarters for his hired hands. The structure was moved three times. In the first move, eight oxen towed the house to a new location. In 1927, it was moved again and restored, and in 1951, it was brought to its present site.

The house has thrived on constant use. Thirty-two children have been raised within its walls, and while it is primarily in its original state, it has been carefully altered to include twentieth-century conveniences to allow for contemporary living. The wall between the living room and the dining room (formerly the lean-to kitchen) has been removed to make an L-shaped living–dining area. Off the dining room, a few steps lead down into a new kitchen–family room.

Opposite: In the living area, the brilliant reds in upholstery, draperies, and Oriental rugs accent the rich patina of the old paneled walls and antique furniture.

Above: The L-shaped living-dining room. Off the dining area, a few steps lead down into a new kitchen–family room.

Left: A red-and-white quilt in "Drunkard's Path" design covers the bed in this room. The canopy, depicting the three moves of the house to varying locations, was embroidered by the lady of the house. A trundle bed slides under the large bed. An eighteenth-century toile de Jouy hangs on the wall.

Page 23: In the kitchen–family room, traditional elements are combined with twentieth-century conveniences.

25

Buttolph-Williams House
1692, Wethersfield

Massively built, the Buttolph-Williams House in Wethersfield follows in style the English Tudor tradition of building the upper floors to make an overhang on each story. The classic batten entrance door is made of several thicknesses of wood held together by handmade nails set in a diamond pattern. Carved corbels under the overhang provide a decorative architectural touch. The uncovered posts and beams visible in the interior show how sturdily this two-over-two Connecticut Plan house was constructed.

A mansion by Colonial standards, the house was the home of David Buttolph, who built it on land left to him by his father,

Lieutenant John Buttolph, a trader and glove maker who brought his family to Wethersfield in 1676. Although sold soon after it was built, the house continued to be used as a residence by various families for over two hundred and fifty years. In 1947, it was restored under the skillful supervision of the noted restoration architect Frédéric C. Palmer. Alterations made by various occupants were removed, and the house was refurnished with seventeenth-century furniture, utensils, and household equipment. Now owned by the Antiquarian and Landmarks Society of Connecticut, the house has been designated a National Historic Landmark.

Top: Rare English delft plate depicting William of Orange.
Center: Sewing basket.
Bottom: A posset bowl, from which hot drinks were drunk through the spout.

28

Opposite above: The "great hall" or parlor. The huge fireplace with its bulbous bolection moldings is similar to English chimney pieces of the Jacobean and Elizabethan periods. *Opposite right:* The hall chamber. Wooden beams showing through aging whitewash have a pinkish tone. The bed has a rose-pink quilt and hangings and flame-stitched valance.

Above: The chamber over the kitchen has not been architecturally altered. The walls were once whitewashed, but the beams have mellowed to a soft beige. *Right:* Glass bottle.

Page 27: "Ye greate kitchin" with its unusual curved settle is an excellent example of its period. A brass spit in the fireplace was found in the attic. Plates and bowls silhouetted against the whitewashed walls are hand-carved treenware.

Michael Griswold House

1680 and 1730, Wethersfield

The Michael Griswold House was begun in 1680 with the large kitchen as its nucleus. The rest of the house was constructed fifty years later.

Michael Griswold, a mason, was an early settler in Wethersfield and owned land there perhaps as early as 1640. When he died in 1684, his home property was left to his wife with the understanding it was thence to go to his son Michael, who was born in 1666. In 1710, Michael Griswold II was commissioned by Governor Gurdon Saltonstall as an ensign in the South Trainband in Wethersfield; the settlers were organized in groups and received military training to fight the Indians, who were a constant threat to their security. Ensign Griswold held various posts of importance in the town and died in 1742. Through the centuries, members of the Griswold family have continued to live in the house, which is now owned by the Griswold Family Association.

Above: The fireplace in what is now the parlor has an oven behind a paneled door.

Opposite: A corner cupboard, original to the house but removed for a time, was reinstalled in the dining room in the twentieth century.

Page 31: The original part of the house is now a sitting room. The mantel is made of a single great timber.

Jonathan Trumbull House

1740, Lebanon

In the latter half of the eighteenth century, Lebanon, a quiet village today, was humming with the traffic and activity of a population larger than that of Hartford. Governor Jonathan Trumbull (1710–1785) was the towering force that guided Connecticut through the critical years that marked its end as an English colony and its beginning as one of the original thirteen states of the new Union. He was governor for more than fourteen and one-half years before, during, and after the Revolutionary War, and his influence contributed substantially to the American victory. As George Washington noted in his diary, "Except for Jonathan Trumbull, the war could not have been carried to a successful conclusion."

Trumbull was educated at Harvard and trained for the ministry, but home circumstances made it necessary for him to go into his father's mercantile business. During the Revolutionary War, his little two-room store became a War Office, and here the Council of Safety met to plan Connecticut's part in the nation's supply efforts. An underground passage between Trumbull's house and the office made it possible to move privately from one to the other.

Jonathan's youngest son, John, also educated at Harvard, studied painting in England under Benjamin West and became America's most famous painter of historic scenes.

The Trumbull house was built by Jonathan Trumbull's father, Captain Joseph Trumbull, a merchant shipowner with a thriving overseas trade. It is a splendid example of Connecticut's architecture as it advanced from the two-over-two beamed construction to the lighter, larger, many-windowed buildings of the eighteenth century. During this transition period, houses became more spacious, more open; the Trumbull house has nine rooms. The typical entrance hall in these later houses was no longer a snug little space with a cramped dog-leg stairway, but a broader, longer passage running through the center of the house with a straighter staircase at one side. To one side of the hall was the front parlor; behind it, the back parlor. At the other side were the dining room and a large kitchen. There were back additions, sheds, and barns. From the kitchen there was another stairway to the second floor, where there were four bedrooms and Governor Jonathan Trumbull's office. John Trumbull fell on these back stairs when he was a boy, damaging the sight of one eye. As a result, most of his paintings are small—twenty-by-thirty-inch canvases—although those commissioned by President James Madison for the rotunda of the Capitol and several life-size portraits of George Washington are much larger.

The house is now owned by the Connecticut Daughters of the American Revolution.

Right: Portrait of Jonathan Trumbull by John Trumbull. (Courtesy Wadsworth Atheneum, Hartford.)

Above left: The kitchen. The woodwork is painted, in Colonial fashion, in the soft gray-blue hue of blueberries crushed in buttermilk.

Above right: Corner fireplace in one of the bedrooms.

Left: A hooked woolen bed rug covers the bed in a front bedroom.

Oliver Ellsworth Homestead

1740, Windsor

Oliver Ellsworth (1745–1807), delegate to the Continental Congress and second Chief Justice of the Supreme Court of the United States, described Elmwood as "the pleasantest place in Windsor." It is the house in which he was born and raised and where he said he would be "content to die." The larger part of the house was built by his father, Captain David Ellsworth, a veteran of the French and Indian Wars, on land that had been in the famly since 1655. When Oliver Ellsworth took over the house, he added an imposing new wing that included a formal drawing room with a large state bedroom above it. He also planted thirteen elms—one for each state of the new Union—and renamed the estate Elmwood. The property came to Oliver Ellsworth after his widowed mother married Ebenezer Grant (page 70) in 1784. A corner cupboard from the Grant House is now in the breakfast room of Elmwood.

Oliver Ellsworth was educated at Yale and Princeton. He prepared for the ministry, but then turned to law and was admitted to the Connecticut bar in 1771. He married Abigail Wolcott in 1772 and started a successful practice in Hartford but his career soon expanded from local to national importance.

Ellsworth, Roger Sherman, and William Samuel Johnson were Connecticut's delegates to the Constitutional Convention, and it was Ellsworth and Sherman who resolved the disagreement over the question of representation by proposing the "Connecticut Compromise" of 1787, which provided for a federal legislature of two houses. Ellsworth was also one of the principal authors of the Judiciary Act of 1789, which established the federal court system, and of the Constitution of the United States.

As one of Connecticut's first two senators, Oliver Ellsworth became a strong Federalist spokesman and in 1796 George Washington appointed him Chief Justice of the Supreme Court. President John Adams sent Ellsworth, William Vans Murray (1762–1803), and William R. Davie (1756–1820) to negotiate a treaty with France in 1799. Ellsworth resigned from the Supreme Court in 1800. He worked to remodel the Connecticut judiciary and was appointed Chief Justice of the Connecticut Supreme Court in 1807.

The Ellsworth Homestead was deeded to the Connecticut Daughters of the American Revolution by the Ellsworth heirs in 1903 and is maintained by the Ellsworth Memorial Association of the DAR as a historic landmark and museum. The Ellsworth heirlooms with which it is furnished have been supplemented by gifts of antiques from members of the Connecticut DAR and their friends.

Left: The formal parlor. The tea service, sofa, and one of the chairs are Ellsworth heirlooms.

Above: Wallpaper that Ellsworth brought back from France still covers the walls of his bedroom.
Right: Oliver Ellsworth and Abigail Woolcott Ellsworth in a painting by Ralph Earl. A view of Elmwood is seen through the window. (Courtesy Wadsworth Atheneum, Hartford.)
Opposite: Corner cupboard in the breakfast room.

Ezekiel Phelps House

1744, Hartford County

Three Phelps houses are shown in this book: those of Ezekiel, Elisha (page 96), and Arah (page 112). The houses were built at different dates and in different towns, but Ezekiel, Elisha, and Arah were all fifth-generation descendants of William Phelps, who in 1630 left Plymouth, England, for Dorchester, Massachusetts, with a group led by the Reverend John Warham. William Phelps became a freeman on October 19, 1630, and in the spring of 1636 he and his five children joined Warham's followers in their new settlement in Windsor.

Ezekiel's father, Joseph Phelps, built this house as a wedding gift for young Ezekiel and his bride, Elizabeth Gillette. Ezekiel and Elizabeth had twelve children, and Joel, one of the younger sons, inherited the house and barns in 1781. Seven years later Joel sold the property to Samuel Clark, who in 1828 left an estate of over $20,000. Clark's children lived here until 1839, when the farm was bought by Raynor Holcomb, whose descendants lived in the house until the present owners bought it in 1959.

Through the years the Ezekiel Phelps House was remodeled by various occupants, but its original style has been reinstated by the present owners. They have added essential conveniences, but the basic shell, the original paneling, fireplaces, and beamed ceilings have been rescued from layers of plaster and Victorian fixtures and trim and lovingly restored to their original condition.

Above: Corner of one of the bedrooms.
Right: A portrait of Samuel Clark hangs above an antique chest.

Page 43: The dining room has sage green woodwork, red draperies, and an Oriental rug. Pewterware gleams on the table.

Above: The fireplace in what was once the kitchen is equipped with eighteenth-century utensils. The chair at left is of Dutch or German origin. The lintel over the hearth is one long piece of stone.

Left: A primitive weathervane of fine design.

Wrightwood

c. 1680–1700, 1727, and 1830, Middlesex County

This beautiful family home was begun sometime in the last two decades of the seventeenth century. The original homestead was a one-room structure, probably with a lean-to addition. A staircase led to an attic chamber above. There were substantial additions to the house in 1727, and again in about 1830. The house has passed from generation to generation by inheritance. From 1914, it was

used by the James H. Wrights as a summer home. In 1970–1971, their son, Dr. James H. Wright, and his family renovated it for year-round living. Major restoration was done then, and the tremendous original fireplace, the paneling, the oak summer beam, and the chestnut cross beams were uncovered. The house is furnished with things old and new, many of the pieces being family heirlooms.

Opposite above: In the older part of the house, a seventeenth-century fireplace has a beehive oven and a lug pole with notched and chain trammels to adjust the height of cooking pots. Vertical-planked walls have feather-and-bead joints.

Opposite : Pewterware is arranged on a shelf in the dining room and blue-and-white Canton ware is displayed in a hutch cabinet.
Above: Victorian pieces blend with heirlooms of an earlier period in the parlor.

Page 47: An early tavern table and chairs, a secretary desk, a family portrait, a Russian samovar made into a lamp, and a European chest combine harmoniously in this room.

Glebe House

1745–1750, Woodbury

Glebe House sits in a hollow behind the white clapboard houses of Woodbury's Main Street. Here, a few steps away from the town's throbbing traffic, is a bit of country quiet with a few ancient houses set in open meadowlands amid wide-girthed trees. The unhurried stillness recalls the atmosphere of the times when Glebe House was built.

The name Glebe indicates, of course, that the house was used as a parsonage and endowed with lands to support the clergyman and his family. At the time of the Revolutionary War, the resident clergyman was John Rutgers Marshall (1743–1789), rector of St. Paul's Parish in Woodbury and father of nine children. After the war, the Church of England was in bitter disfavor, and the persecution of Reverend Marshall became so intense that he could not leave his house unmolested. Legend says that he consequently had a tunnel built from his house to a nearby store.

The break with England soon brought about a break with the Church of England as well. As the church had no bishops in America (Anglican priests had always gone to London for ordination), there was no one available to ordain new ministers. To remedy the matter, ten of the fourteen Episcopal clergymen in Connecticut met at Glebe House on March 25, 1783, and selected the Reverend Samuel Seabury (1729–1796), a descendant of John Alden, as their bishop. Their act established Glebe House as the birthplace of the Episcopal Church in America, for the first interstate conventions to draft a new constitution for the denomination did not begin until the following year. In 1784, Samuel Seabury, having given up hope of ordination in London because he would not take the required oath of allegiance to the king, went to Scotland for consecration. He thus became the church's first bishop, and in 1789 he was selected as presiding bishop for the United States.

Glebe House, an enlarged version of a Connecticut two-over-two house with added lean-to at the back, was expanded from a smaller structure built about 1690. There is a small bedroom and storage space over the lean-to, and in the attic under the gambrel roof there is a smokehouse flued into the central chimney. The sycamore tree at the side of the house is said to be over three hundred years old.

In 1786, the house was sold to provide funds to finance the building of the present church building, but was repurchased by friends of the church in 1892. Since 1925, the house has been in the care of the Seabury Society for the Preservation of the Glebe House.

The Reverend Samuel Seabury, from a 1786 engraving by William Sharp after the painting by Thomas Spence Duche. The Glebe House, Gift of Miss Grace Scoville.

Above: The great kitchen.
Right: An indigo blue calamanco quilt made by Mrs. John Rutgers Marshall covers the bed in one of the bedrooms.
Opposite: In the parlor where Samuel Seabury was elected bishop, the wing chair he sat in still has its original covering.

Joseph Webb House

1752, Wethersfield

This house was built in 1752 by Joseph Webb Sr. (1727–1761), a fifth-generation Webb in this country, and a well-to-do merchant who owned his own sailing vessels and operated a lucrative trade with the West Indies as well as a store in Wethersfield. At twenty-one, he married Mehitabel Nott, daughter of Gershem Nott, a wealthy sea captain and descendant of John Nott, one of the first settlers in Wethersfield. Four years later Webb bought the property on which this substantial mansion-house stands.

Joseph Webb died in 1761, leaving a wife and six children. Two years after his death his widow married Silas Deane (page 90), who built a new home for her next door. The older children continued to live in the house their father had built, with Joseph Jr. and Samuel Blanchley, then only twelve and eight years old, taking on adult responsibilities. Young Joseph continued his father's business and also became a successful merchant. During the Revolutionary War, he helped to commission clothing, food, and supplies for the army, was made a commissioner for the Continental Loan funds, and aided the widows and children of the town's soldiers lost in battle.

Joseph Jr. married Abigail Chester, daughter of Colonel John Chester, and a descendant of the Thomas Hooker family. Abigail Chester Webb was famed as a charming hostess and Webb House soon became known as "Hospitality Hall." George Washington enjoyed the Webbs' hospitality in May 1781, when he met with the Comte de Rochambeau and the French commanders in a five-day conference at which they planned strategy for the decisive battle at Yorktown. Washington wrote in his account book that he had spent 35 pounds, 18 shillings for the Wethersfield journey "for the purpose of an interview with the French General and Admiral."

Webb House and Silas Deane House on one side and the house of boot and shoemaker Isaac Stevens on the other form a three-house museum complex that affords interesting insight into eighteenth-century domestic arrangements at different social and income levels. The famed antiquarian Wallace Nutting (1861–1941), who once lived in Webb House, called it "a shrine and monument." All three houses are owned by the National Society of the Colonial Dames of America in the State of Connecticut, who have painstakingly restored and furnished the houses and maintain them as museums.

The bedroom used by George Washington when he stayed with the Webbs in Wethersfield.

54

Above: The parlor where George Washington met with Rochambeau to plan the Battle of Yorktown.

Detail of the design of the cinnamon-brown flock wallpaper that was purchased especially for General Washington's visit.

Left: Chinese Export porcelain is arranged on butterfly shelves in a polychrome cupboard in the ladies' parlor.
Above: Chinese Export punch bowl.

Below: The dining room. The paneled wall is painted slate blue.

Abijah Rowe and Enders-Weed Houses

c. 1753 and c. 1790, Granby

The tree-shaded two-story Abijah Rowe House was built at its present location on Salmon Brook Street in Granby; the adjoining small saltbox Enders-Weed House was moved here from a site six miles away in what is now the Enders State Forest. The smaller building provides office and library space for the Salmon Brook Historical Society and serves as well as an example of a farmhouse of its period.

Abijah Rowe was a farmer and blacksmith and must have been reasonably successful, for the house is a substantial one. The blacksmiths of his day not only shod horses; they made carpenters' tools, farm equipment, nails, hinges, locks, door handles, fireplace cranes and andirons, weathervanes, and whaling harpoons. Abijah Rowe died in 1813

and the house was sold to Joseph and Elijah Smith Jr. It later served to house workers on the tobacco farm of Fred M. Colton, who bought the house in 1903. His heirs, Caroline Colton Avery and Mildred Colton Allison, presented it to the Salmon Brook Historical Society in 1966. Now restored, the house has been refurnished with antiques, many of which, though not original to the house, are from the Granby area.

The Enders-Weed House was originally the home of a family named Weed; it then passed into the hands of families named Lampson (in 1857) and Corell (in 1919). Its use as a family farmhouse finally came to an end; John Enders, who bought the house in the 1920s, used it as a hunting cabin.

Above: Parlor chamber in the Abijah Rowe House.
Right: Wall box.

Page 59: Dining room of the Rowe House. A rare Stiegel glass pitcher stands on the table and a blue-and-white Delft plate hangs over the mantel.

Above: Corner fireplace in the Enders-Weed House.

Left: The compact kitchen of the Rowe House. The basket in front of the settle was used for plucking geese. The tapered opening confined the down.

61

Wells-Shipman-Ward House

1755, South Glastonbury

This magnificent house was built by a wealthy shipbuilder, Thomas Wells, for his son John Wells at the time of his marriage. The structure has been owned by three different families. The last owner was Mrs. James Ward, who willed it to the Historical Society of Glastonbury.

An outstanding example of mid-eighteenth-century Connecticut River Valley architecture, the house has a formal herb garden at the back with brick walks and a luxurious array of herbs. During the seventeenth and eighteenth centuries, when herbs were used for seasonings and herb teas, for dyeing yarns and fabrics, and for medicinal purposes, a substantial herb garden was a valuable asset.

Many hands have helped in refurnishing the house in an appropriate style. Chippendale-style chairs in the Northwest Parlor, for instance, were hand-carved in 1936 by Nathan Margolis, a craftsman who specialized in reproducing eighteenth-century furniture. The brightly colored chair seats were embroidered by members of the Connecticut River Valley Chapter of the Embroiderers' Guild of America, following designs created by Muriel Baker and inspired by museum examples of the period. The eighteenth-century cherry secretary, Connecticut made, is on loan from Mrs. Aaron W. Kinne.

Above left: The herb garden.
Above right: The borning room off the kitchen.
Right: Doll in crewel-embroidered dress.

Page 63: A corner of the Northwest Parlor. Paneled shutters, original to the house, slide in recessed grooves. Crown moldings decorate the encased summer beam and cornice.

The front entrance.

Above: A corner of the Red Parlor. John Wells' initials in Greek and the date 1755 are chalked on the fireplace lintel. The tall clock was made in Connecticut.

Weatherstone

1765, Sharon

Larger and more commodious than most eighteenth-century Connecticut houses, Weatherstone is believed to have been built by a Genoese architect with imported labor for Dr. Simeon Smith (1733–1804) in 1765. Dr. Smith was a fifth-generation descendant of Henry Smith (1588–1648), who came to Massachusetts from Norwich, England, in 1637, and in 1639 became the first "settled pastor" of Wethersfield.

Dr. Simeon Smith was educated abroad and began to practice medicine in Connecticut about 1759. As he became wealthy, he invested in tremendous land holdings in Connecticut and Vermont. His large mansion-house was started in 1765, but not completed until after the Revolutionary War. Dr. Smith suffered severe losses in the lean times

after the war, and his brother, the Reverend Cotton Mather Smith (1730–1806), took over Weatherstone. Except for a very brief interlude in the years since, the house has been owned and lived in by nine generations of the Smith family. Mr. and Mrs. John H. Spencer are the present owners of Weatherstone; Mr. Spencer is descended from Julia Radcliff Spencer, granddaughter of Cotton Mather Smith and daughter of Juliana Smith Radcliff and Jacob Radcliff, who was mayor of New York in 1810 and again in 1815–1817.

Noah Webster stayed at Weatherstone for a time while working on his *American Spelling Book;* the house was then the home of John Cotton Smith (1765–1845), who was governor of Connecticut 1815–1817.

Above: The formal drawing room. Hand-painted blue-and-white wall-paper is a copy of an eighteenth-century design. A George I sofa and eighteenth-century chairs are covered with yellow silk damask.

Right: Portrait of Jacob Radcliff by John Trumbull.

Far right: The bed in the white-walled master bedroom is festooned with white hangings. Salmon pink chintz on the chairs and tables adds a strong note of color.

Above: The living room. Above the sofa is a portrait of William Radcliff, father of Jacob Radcliff, by Rembrandt Peale.

Left: The dining room. The table is set with early-eighteenth-century blue-and-white Worcester china and Georgian candlesticks. Needlepoint screen panels were made by Mrs. Spencer's grandmother, Mrs. T. W. Bunte of Chicago, in her eighty-ninth year.

Page 67: Window bay in the dining room is the backdrop for a Chippendale pagoda display cabinet. Swagged cotton curtains are copies of ones designed for Monticello by Thomas Jefferson.

Ebenezer Grant House

1757, Hartford County

With its superb front entrance and fine architectural details, the Ebenezer Grant House is one of the handsomest houses in New England, a fitting residence for the wealthy merchant who built it. Ebenezer Grant (1706–1797), great-uncle of President Ulysses S.. Grant, was a fourth-generation Grant in this country. His first forebear here, Matthew Grant, came to Dorchester, Massachusetts, with the Reverend John Warham and others of his congregation, and in 1635 followed Warham to Connecticut. There he became town clerk, selectman, and surveyor of his community and kept detailed records of its progress.

Matthew's great-grandson Ebenezer also kept records, including a detailed account of his domestic arrangements and of brisk trading and shipping ventures with Boston and the West Indies. His house must have been handsomely furnished; in 1775, he purchased from the famous cabinetmaker Eliphalet Chapin (1741–1807): "2 large dining tables; 2 candle stands; 1 hand table; 1 bed cornice; 1 breakfast table; 1 screen frame; 2 armed chairs; 2 cherry bedsteads, long posts, claws; two doz. claw feet cherry chairs, etc. for £41-13-0." Some of these furnishings may have been for the home of his daughter Ann.

Ebenezer Grant's first wife was Ann Elsworth. Of their children, only two lived: Roswell, a son, and Ann, who married the Reverend John Marsh, pastor of the Wethersfield church. When George Washington dined at the Joseph Webb House during his stay in Wethersfield in May 1781, the Reverend and Mrs. Marsh were among the guests.

At the age of seventy-eight, after his first wife died, Ebenezer married Jemima Leavitt Ellsworth, mother of Chief Justice Oliver Ellsworth (page 38). Grant fought in the French and Indian War, raised supplies for the Continental Army during the Revolutionary War, and lived to be ninety-one years old.

Ebenezer Grant's house stands on the same site as one built by his grandfather, Samuell Grant, in 1695. When he built this great mansion-house, Ebenezer thriftily preserved the old two-story structure as an ell at the back. Changes were made in the house in 1911, and the furnishings were sold, but the present owners have been enthusiastically restoring it to its former elegance.

Below: Detail of the stairway.
Right: An early account desk.
Opposite: The dining room.

Noah Webster House

c. 1700, West Hartford

A great deal of American history is represented in the simple Connecticut Plan farmhouse that was the birthplace of Noah Webster (1758–1843). On the maternal side, Noah Webster was descended from William Bradford, second governor of the Plymouth colony and documentarian of the Plymouth Plantation from 1620 to 1647. Noah's father was descended from John Webster, one of Thomas Hooker's followers and governor of Connecticut in 1656.

Webster's Puritan family background influenced his life work. He realized the need for cultural as well as political freedom and hoped that his work would encourage morals and patriotism as well as improve language.

His *American Spelling Book* (1783), later incorporated into *A Grammatical Institution of the English Language* (1783–1785), became the standard guide to spelling and composition for generations of schoolchildren. *A Compendious Dictionary of the English Language* (1807) and *A Philosophical and Practical Grammar of the English Language* were forerunners of his great *American Dictionary of the English Language*, which he finished (working in France and England) in 1824–1825 and finally published in 1828. In order to bring a depth of understanding to his work, he mastered many languages. He also wrote papers on political, literary, and moral topics, established newspapers and a magazine, taught, lectured, wrote on and campaigned for copyright laws to protect American authors, practiced law, served in the Connecticut legislature, and, like all people of his era, at times also managed the family farm. Shortly before his death in New Haven in 1843, Webster finished revising the appendix to the second edition of his great dictionary; at eighty-five, he had lived long enough to see the impact of his contribution to American cultural life.

A frugal man, at the beginning of his marriage to Rebecca Greenleaf he promised with New England practicality that if they did not quarrel in their first year, he would give her, not a diamond ring or brooch, or a few yards of silk for a gown, but a "flitch of bacon." The year must have passed happily, for Rebecca won the bacon.

Begun early in the eighteenth century, probably as a two-room, two-story structure with a side chimney, by the time of Noah Webster's birth the family home had been expanded into the two-over-two Connecticut Plan house shown here. In 1787, a lean-to was added at the back, and to this an ell was appended some time during the nineteenth century. A National Historic Landmark, the house is in the care of the Noah Webster Foundation and the Historical Society of West Hartford. It has been restored and refurnished to appear as it might have been when Webster was born in 1758.

The kitchen. A small brick oven is built into the back of the wide fireplace.

Above: The parlor.
Opposite above : The parlor chamber has a fine carved chest, a canopied bed, and a long cradle.

76

Above: The chamber over the kitchen is equipped for spinning and weaving.

Sheldon's Tavern

1760 and 1790, Litchfield County

Originally built in 1760 by Elisha Sheldon, this imposing white clapboard house was later converted into an inn by his son, and it has been called Sheldon's Tavern ever since, even though it is now a private home. In 1790, Uriah Tracy, who was then the owner, commissioned William Spratt (1757–1810) to renovate the house. It was Spratt (or Sprats, as he frequently signed his name) who added the projecting front entrance and portico, the handsome Palladian window, and the mansard roof.

Although not much is known of Spratt's personal life, tradition says that he defected from Burgoyne's army and was captured by the Americans and imprisoned in the Hartford area. After the Revolutionary War he remained in New England and designed some of the most outstanding Georgian-style buildings there. Innumerable examples of his work from the immediate postwar period, including public buildings and private dwellings, are to be found in Connecticut. In the early 1790s, he moved from Milton, Connecticut, to Whitehall, New York, where he died at the age of fifty-three. Fine examples of his work may also be found in that area and in neighboring Vermont, where he is buried in the West Haven cemetery not far from Simeon Smith (page 66).

The character of his designs shows that Spratt must have been familiar with the work of Inigo Jones (1543–1651) and Christopher Wren (1632–1723). Jones' four-volume *The Architecture of Palladio* was published in 1715, and *The Designs of Inigo Jones,* by William Kent, appeared in 1757. No doubt Spratt had these or similar references at hand. He may also have been acquainted with the works of the prominent New England architects Charles Bulfinch (1763–1844), who designed the State Houses in Hartford (1796) and Boston (1795–1798), and Asher Benjamin (1773–1845), who published books of plans that were widely copied by other architects.

Spratt's use of columns, pilasters, balustrades, Palladian windows, bold dentil friezes, quoins, and pediments give his exterior and interior architecture elegance and importance. His sense of proportion was magnificent, bold rather than delicate.

The front entrance bay designed by William Spratt.

Above left: The front parlor has clay-orange walls, blue-and-white delft tiles around the fireplace opening, and deep blue tones in the Chinese rug.

Above right: A portion of the entrance hall.

Opposite below: **A full view of the house shows the design of Spratt's mansard roof and balustrade.**

Above: Paneled walls in the present dining room are painted hyacinth blue. Tall windows flood the room with light.

Alexander King House

1764, Suffield

Dr. Alexander King (1737–1802), whose great-grandfather had come to Suffield in 1678, graduated from Yale in 1759 and returned to Suffield to practice medicine. One year before his marriage he built this house on land his father, grandfather, and great-grandfather had owned; it served as both his home and his office. The porch on the south is original and leads to the door his patients used to reach his office in the south ell. From 1768 to 1784, Dr. King was a member of the Connecticut General Assembly and in 1788 he was a member of the state convention called to ratify the Constitution. In 1793, he sold the house to his cousin, Horace King.

The house was purchased in 1910 by Mr. and Mrs. Samuel Reid Spencer, who restored and refurnished it with eighteenth- and early-nineteenth-century antiques, and then presented it to the Suffield Historical Society. Although the house had several owners between the time it was sold by Horace King in 1869 and purchased by the Spencers in 1910, the interior was unchanged. Except for the ell that housed the doctor's office, the plan is a typical one for its period. Two large rooms flank the entrance, a large kitchen with a "borning-room" at one side runs across the back of the house, and a large center chimney serves all the fireplaces.

Above: In the parlor chamber, a bed from the Jonathan Trumbull House has been dressed with crewel-embroidered linen from Scalamandre in England.

Above right: The dining room. The side tables were made in 1809 by John Fitch Parsons of Suffield and the built-in cupboard is believed to be the work of the Suffield cabinet-maker and builder Eliphalet King.

Right: This rare dining-room over-mantel painting of an English rural scene has been attributed to Dr. King's son Charles, who studied with Isaac Sanford of Hartford.

Opposite: The wide kitchen fireplace.

George King House

1769 and 1794–1797, Sharon

Except for a brief period, this gambrel-roofed brick house with its generous dormers and large Palladian window above the columned portico has always been in the hands of one family. In 1783, George King of Windsor bought a one-room structure with a large fireplace that had been built on the site in 1769 by John Pennoyer. In 1794, King began building the present house around this single large room. Successive generations of the King family lived there until 1906, when the house was sold. In 1924, it was purchased by Mrs. Caroline B. Hart, the great-great-grand-daughter of George King, and her husband, the late Admiral (and state senator) Thomas C. Hart. Mrs. Hart has refurnished the house with many of its original pieces. The old Pennoyer structure, at first used as a kitchen, is now a dining room, and the rest of the house has been restored.

Above: The hallway, looking toward the rear of the house.

Right: The former kitchen is now the dining room.

Opposite: A bedroom on the ground floor.

Page 87: The library was added to the rear of the house in 1925. A wide terrace opening off it offers a view of the surrounding hills and forests.

Silas Deane House

1766, Wethersfield

Silas Deane (1737–1789), son of a Groton blacksmith, went to Yale, then studied law in Hartford. He was admitted to the bar in 1761 and began to practice his profession in Wethersfield. That same year the prosperous merchant Joseph Webb (page 54) died at thirty-four, leaving a thriving business, a wealthy widow, and six children. Deane became Mehitabel Nott Webb's legal adviser, and in 1763 they were married. Deane gradually decreased his law practice, and became increasingly active in trade with the West Indies. In 1766, he built this grand house next to the Webb House. Mehitabel Deane died in

1767, leaving a small son by Deane and her six children by Joseph Webb. Deane closed out his dealings with the West Indies that same year.

Three years later, Silas Deane married the socially prominent Elizabeth Saltonstall, granddaughter of a past governor of Connecticut, Gurdon Saltonstall. Deane became Wethersfield's representative in the General Assembly of Connecticut and clerk to the Connecticut Committee of Correspondence. As a member of the assembly, he conceived the plan to attack Ticonderoga and supported the funding of Ethan Allen's expedi-

The dining room.

tion by the Connecticut treasury. With Roger Sherman and Eliphalet Dyer, he represented the colony at the Continental Congress. Early in 1776, he was sent to France, first as a secret agent and later as regularly accredited commissioner, to seek financial aid and secure military supplies and to work out a treaty of alliance and trade. Benjamin Franklin and Arthur Lee joined him there. Deane was recalled in November 1777, but stayed in Paris to conclude the treaties of alliance in February 1778 before coming home. He went back to Paris in 1781, and from there went to Holland, and thence to England, after the treaty of peace with England was signed. He died in England in 1789 just as he was about to return to America.

A National Historic Landmark, Silas Deane's elegantly furnished house is owned and maintained by the National Society of the Colonial Dames of America in the State of Connecticut.

Opposite: In the kitchen, a brass clock jack installed above the fireplace controls the action of the spit. *Above:* The front parlor arranged for entertaining. A portrait of Silas Deane by William Johnston hangs on the wall. When not in use, this "best parlor" was kept closed and the furniture was lined up along the walls.
Left: Pewter teapot.

Above: The back parlor or smoking room.
Right: Delft plate.

Left: This silver coffeepot made by Samuel Buell of Middletown and Hartford is the only known existing eighteenth-century Connecticut-made example.

Above: Woodwork the color of a dried bayleaf outlines white plaster walls in the front parlor-chamber. An eighteenth-century Oriental rug is on the floor. Curtains and upholstery are a blue-and-white resist fabric.

Elisha Phelps Tavern

1771, Simsbury

Captain Elisha Phelps (1737–1776) was a merchant in Simsbury at the time he built this house. He was appointed captain by Governor Trumbull in May 1774 and was later designated commissary for the Connecticut troops in the Northern Department. He died at Albany in 1776 and his son inherited the homestead. Descendants of the family continued to live in the house until 1969, when it was bequeathed to the Simsbury Historical Society.

After the War of 1812, the house was operated as a tavern and hotel until 1850. The Society has furnished it as it might have been when travelers using the North Hampton Canal would stop for a meal or overnight lodging to break the twenty-four-hour journey from New Haven to North Hampton.

Additions and alterations to the house were made by various Phelps occupants over the years. A grand ballroom on the second floor (considered to be one of the grandest of its period) was added in 1806. Its domed canvas ceiling is still in remarkably good condition. A handsome wing added in 1879 includes a large dining room. Among its appointments is part of a commemorative set of Staffordshire dinnerware; the other half of the set is in the Metropolitan Museum of Art in New York.

The house is part of a complex of buildings in what is known as Massacoh (or Massacoe) Plantation. There were settlers here as early as 1664, although the town of Simsbury was not incorporated until 1670. Massacoh was the Indian name for this region along the Farmington River.

Left: The compact entrance hall has a dog-leg staircase.
Below: Worcester and Staffordshire blue-and-white ware in a wall cupboard in the dining room.
Below left: Signboard from the period when the house served as a tavern.

Page 96: In the kitchen, an old settle hugs the warmth of the hearth.

Above: The taproom. A spoked gate swings down to enclose the bar. Plaster walls are whitewashed, and woodwork and paneling are painted a bright leaf green.

Left: Cupboards above the taproom hearth store pewter plate. A checkerboard rests on a wooden crate. Behind the comb-backed Windsor chair, a pipe box holds a clay pipe.

Gay-Hoyt House

1775–1776, Sharon

One of eleven children, Lieutenant-Colonel Ebenezer Gay was born in Litchfield and moved to Sharon in 1743 with his parents. He served his community in many capacities—as a tax collector, as a five-term representative from Sharon to the General Assembly, on active service in the Revolutionary War, and in gathering arms, food, and clothing for the army. He also operated a store on the Main Street lot where he built this salmon pink brick house, but the war was hard on his finances, as it was on those of most of the people of the colonies. Ill health forced him to resign his commission in 1783; he died insolvent in 1787, and the house was sold. Miss Anne Sherman Hoyt, who bought the house in 1936, bequeathed it to the Sharon Historical Society, which now maintains it as a museum.

Above: The table is set for tea in front of the corner fireplace in the front parlor.

Page 101: Slender columns support the archway joining the front and back parlors.

Above: A bow window adjoining the back entrance was formerly the display window of a milliner's shop.

Left: A portrait of John Cotton Smith (1765–1845), governor of Connecticut 1815–1817, hangs over a console table in the back parlor.

Oldgate

c. 1786, Farmington

This regal handsomely proportioned yellow clapboard house was the first of the American houses built by William Spratt. When he drew the plans, Spratt incorporated at the back a section built about 1660 for William Hooker (1663–1695), son of the Reverend Samuel Hooker. The property passed through several hands before it was taken over by Captain Solomon Cowles in 1782 and rebuilt in its present form for his son Zenas. The actual construction work is believed to have been done by prisoners from New-Gate Prison in East Granby. Additions to the house were made in 1900 by Rear Admiral William Sheffield Cowles and his wife, Anna Roosevelt Cowles, sister of President Theodore Roosevelt.

Oldgate was named for its handsome entrance gate, which was inspired by a watergate on the Thames designed by Christopher Wren. The Palladian window, with its crowning pediment and exquisite dentil frieze, the corner quoins, the architectural details of the broad halls and spacious rooms, and the magnificent fireplaces make this house one of the great architectural triumphs of Connecticut, and indeed of the United States. The house has been owned by members of the Cowles family ever since it was rebuilt. The present owners are Mr. and Mrs. William Sheffield Cowles.

Above: The upstairs hall, now used as the owner's office, has an original Duncan Phyfe sofa at the right.

Right: Library in the seventeenth-century part of the house. The brick fireplace is original, but the wide contemporary window adds light and a view of the garden.

Above: The hallway showing the encased staircase at the rear and the dentil cornice.
Above right: The entrance gate.

Page 105: The dining room. William Spratt's architectural details, in white, stand out dramatically against vivid green walls. The portrait is of Admiral William Sheffield Cowles. The dining table originally was owned by Archibald Bullock, a Maryland delegate to the Continental Congress.

Cheney Homestead

1784, Manchester

Cheney is an old name in New England; a John and Martha Cheney came to this country in 1635, settling first in Roxbury and then in Newbury, Massachusetts. The first known Cheney in Connecticut was Benjamin, who is known to have purchased land in the colony in 1724. There is no direct record, but there is reason to believe that the Benjamin Cheney who built this house was Benjamin Cheney of Newbury, a great-grandson of John, for the Newbury Cheneys are known to have bought land in Connecticut about this time. Benjamin built a handsome house on East Center Street in Manchester, which has since been bulldozed to make room for an apartment complex, but the house at 106 Hartford Road shown here, built by his son Timothy, has been preserved.

Benjamin Cheney had two sons, Timothy and Benjamin Jr., and both were clockmakers. They made what were probably the first wooden clocks in America, forerunners of what was to become the extensive Connecticut clock industry. Timothy's son George inherited the house in 1795. Three years later he married Electa Deodatus Woodbridge and they had nine children—eight boys and one girl. Two of the boys, Seth and John, were successful artists and engravers. Seth painted portraits of Daniel Webster, Henry Wadsworth Longfellow, and James Russell Lowell; John did engravings for book illustrations. Other sons formed the famous Cheney Brothers Silk Mills; it was the beginning of the state's once-great silk industry. Seth and John also invested in the silk mill, and from his earnings from his engravings, John purchased the beautiful eighteenth- and nine-

teenth-century furniture seen throughout this house.

Set on a hillside, Cheney Homestead is an early example of a split-level house, with one entrance on the east side, which opens into the "best formal parlor," and another at a lower level on the south side, which leads into what was originally the keeping room. A wing was added to the back (or west) side of the house in the early 1800s but the initial form of the house is apparent in the placement of the posts in some of the rooms.

The house is now owned by the Manchester Historical Society. Most of the rooms are open to the public and are furnished much as they were when the Cheney family lived here.

The buttery.

Above left: Eighteenth-century American pieces are grouped around the Franklin stove in the living room.
Above right: A corner of the formal parlor.
Left: Dining room in the nineteenth-century wing was once the dormitory room for George Cheney's eight sons. The chairs are attributed to Eliphalet Chapin, and are the largest known matching set by him. Cheney family portraits hang on the walls.
Opposite: The attic studio is dedicated to the memory of Seth and John Cheney.

111

Arah Phelps Inn

1787, Litchfield County

Captain Arah (or Asa) Phelps (1760–1844) was a fifth-generation descendant of William Phelps of Windsor. His grandfather had left Windsor to settle in Litchfield County. When Captain Phelps returned from service in the Revolutionary War in 1787, he decided to take advantage of the proximity of the family farm to the turnpike that joined Boston, Hartford, and New Haven by building an inn. First he built a sawmill where he prepared the great timbers that were to form his house; one door in the house is hewn from a single solid slab of wood and the plates topping the frame of the house are eight by sixteen inches by thirty-eight feet long. His brother Ezekiel started an iron foundry close by to forge the nails, hinges, locks, and latches. In addition to running the inn, enterprising Arah Phelps also had a shingle mill, a maple grove that produced sugar and syrup, an apple orchard with an adjacent cider mill, a flock of sheep that produced wool for home spinning and weaving, and cows that supplied milk and cream to supply the cheese factory on his flourishing farm.

Although the house was damaged by fire in 1942, much of what was the original inn was untouched. The house was restored in the 1960s by descendants of the original builder; no longer an inn, it is still the home of members of the family.

7

Above left: Lift-lid desk in the taproom.

Above right: The fireplace wall of the taproom. The back posts of the child's chair are worn from its use as a sled in winter.

Right: The inn's sign was done by the itinerant painter William Rice. A lion on one side of the board and an eagle on the other may represent the retreat of Britain and the rise of American freedom. The sign is now on loan to the Hartford Historical Society.

Page 113: The taproom has its original tavern tables and chairs, but the scroll was acquired in Korea by the present owner during his wartime service there.

114

Above: The entrance hall. The door's iron hardware was made by Arah Phelps's older brother Ezekiel.
Left: The ladies' parlor.

Above: A daguerreotype of Arah Phelps taken in 1844.

Allis-Bushnell House

1739 and 1825, Madison

There were three generations of Nathaniel Allises in Madison; the second Nathaniel Allis, born in 1718, married Hannah Scranton in 1739 and presumably built this saltbox house that same year. Originally it was a duplex house divided by a central hall. Each side had a parlor in the front and a kitchen at the rear, with a low-ceilinged chamber above each parlor. Three succeeding generations of the Allis family lived in the house; some minor changes were made in it in 1785.

Heirs of Nathaniel Allis sold the house to Ichabod Lee Scranton in 1825. That same year Scranton sold it to Nathan Bushnell, who made a more commodious second floor

by adding a wing and raising the roof to enlarge the bedrooms. The house was occupied by three generations of Bushnells. During the Civil War, Cornelius Scranton Bushnell, a member of the second generation, was commended by President Abraham Lincoln for his part in financing the construction of the iron-clad battleship *Monitor* after its historic battle with the *Merrimac* at Hampton Roads.

In 1930, the house was acquired from heirs of the Bushnell family by the Madison Historical Society. It now serves as a museum and as the society's headquarters.

Above: A paneled parlor wall is angled to accommodate a chimney that also serves the kitchen fireplace.
Right: Saltbox.

Page 117: Redware plates, pewter measures, a milk pitcher, candle mold, and wooden mortar are arranged on shelves above a tavern table.

Top: Walls and woodwork in this room are painted sage green; the tavern table is set with pewterware.
Above: Blue-and-white Staffordshire teapot.
Left: Victorian parlor in the nineteenth-century wing of the house.

Isaac Stevens House

1788–1789, Wethersfield

Isaac Stevens (1755–1819), a maker of shoes, boots, saddles, and harnesses, built this house for his bride, Sarah Wright. It stands next to Joseph Webb House on Main Street, and is part of the museum complex that includes Silas Deane House. Less pretentious than its neighbors, Isaac Stevens House is an interesting example of how the average citizen lived in the late eighteenth and nineteenth centuries. Despite the contrast in the wealth of the owners, simplicity and good taste are evident in all three houses. The scale is smaller

and the decoration less elaborate in the Isaac Stevens House, but the interior architectural details are similar. The view here shows the house from the garden at the rear. The back is sheathed with wide weatherboards painted red; the sides and front are green clapboard.

When the National Society of Colonial Dames of America in the State of Connecticut acquired the house in 1958 it was still in the hands of the Stevens family. Many of the present furnishings were Stevens family possessions.

Above: Dining room. The table is set for tea. The pole fire screen can be raised or lowered to deflect the heat of the flames.
Right: Child's bedroom.

Page 121: A sunny corner of the kitchen. All the ground-floor rooms have sliding shutters.

Nineteenth-century doll.

Above: A corner of the kitchen. The original iron door is set in the mouth of the oven.

Adam Stanton House

1789–1791, Clinton

Adam Stanton, who came to Clinton from Rhode Island early in the Revolutionary War, built his house on the east side of Clinton Green, on land that had been owned by the Reverend Abraham Pierson, the first rector of Yale College. From 1701 to 1707, the rector taught students in his home here; the college was then still known as the Collegiate School and had its headquarters in Saybrook. When Adam Stanton bought the property, he used some of the beams from Mr. Pierson's 1694 house to support his chimneys and ground floor. Stanton had a general store and ran a salt distillery. His son and grandson lived here throughout their lives, and the house remained in the family until it was bequeathed to the public by its last owner, Lewis E. Stanton, in memory of his brother John, who lived here from 1826 to 1908.

John Stanton's collection of antiques, furniture, and bric-a-brac have been preserved in the house under the terms of his brother's will. Lewis Stanton entrusted the care of the house and the adjoining general store to the Hartford National Bank and Trust Company and in 1919 the house was opened as a museum.

Above: Turtle-back Hitchcock chairs and an elaborately carved sideboard and table in the dining room are nineteenth-century furnishings. *Right:* Passageway between the kitchen and dining room.

Page 125: A slant-back Brewster chair stands in front of the kitchen hearth and old pewterware is displayed on the mantel. Iron pots and implements are original to the house.

Above: On the opposite side of the kitchen is a court cupboard made in Guilford.

Left: Adam Stanton's bedroom has his four-poster bed and the children's trundle bed.

House in Western Connecticut

1790–1793

Its beautifully balanced proportions make this house one of architect-builder William Spratt's finest masterpieces. The Georgian influence seen in his renovations of Sheldon's Tavern (page 78) and his designs for Oldgate (page 104) is also brought forth in full strength here. The projected entranceway with its pillared overhang, the Palladian window and the balustrade beneath it, the corbeling and dentils of the bold pediment framing the fanlight window, make this an imposing façade. The theme struck by the Ionic columns and pilasters of the portico is repeated with great effect in the interior, particularly in the overmantels of the parlors. Other typical Spratt features in this stately three-story house are quoined corners and a mansard roof with decorative railings. Originally built for a wealthy merchant, it is still a private home.

Ionic pilasters and a dentiled cornice in the front hall carry out Spratt's architectural theme.

Above: The left front parlor. The paneling is painted in two shades of griege, as it was when the house was built.

Right: Robin's egg blue fireplace wall, cornice, and dado, and pale peach plaster walls make the right front parlor a pleasantly colorful room.

Above left: In the upstairs hall, furnished as a study, interior details of the Palladian window match those of the exterior.

Above right: A new dining room with a wide bay window was added to the house in the 1930s.

George Cowles House

1802, Farmington

The pillared garden front of this elegant Georgian mansion has a handsome columned portico that shelters a porch that opens off the front parlor and overlooks a wide brick terrace and the gardens. The porch is supported by groined brick arches that form a protected gallery adjoining the terrace. A graceful Palladian window relieves the severity of the massive pediment. Behind the window is a fifteen-by-fifty-foot ballroom with an elliptical vaulted ceiling. The ballroom is reached by a grand staircase that sweeps up-

ward from an entrance hall that is open all the way to the ceiling of the third floor.

The house was a wedding gift to George Cowles (1780–1860) and his bride, Abigail Deming, from his father, Solomon Cowles. A member of the state legislature in 1815 and from 1821 to 1824, George Cowles was instrumental in forming the Farmington Canal Company. Although the house was sold in 1907, it was later purchased by and is now the home of a relative of the Cowles family.

Above left: A small copy of an early Renaissance fountain in Rome overlooks the terrace and gardens. *Above right:* The dining room.

Page 133: The grand staircase in the front hall.

Above: The living room opens onto the porch; the window sash rises up into a space in the wall.

Left: Beneath the groined arches that support the porch are a carousel rooster and a modern sculpture.

135

Hurlbut-Dunham House

1804–1806, Wethersfield

Supervising the construction himself, Captain John Hurlbut (1770–1808) built this house with his share of the profits from an around-the-world voyage aboard the *Neptune*, the first Connecticut ship to circumnavigate the globe. His joy in it was short-lived; by 1810, he and his wife and one of his two daughters were dead and his brother-in-law had taken over the house. When it was built, the house was a relatively unadorned Federal-style structure. Changes were made by Levi Goodwin (1819–1880), a tavern keeper who bought the house in 1852 and married Hurlbut's great-granddaughter, Adelaide Blinn, in 1858. Goodwin added the columned

porch that shades the two sides of the double parlor, lengthening the windows along one side into glass-paned double doors opening onto it. A back ell and the Italianate embellishment of the belvedere and cornice were other Goodwin additions.

The house was purchased in 1879 by Silas W. Robbins, whose granddaughter, Jane Robbins Dunham (1882–1963), bequeathed it with its grounds and furnishings to the Wethersfield Historical Society. The first floor is now used for the society's social and cultural events and as a museum.

Opposite: The front parlor has furniture of the Victorian and Federal periods. Matching marble mantelpieces were installed in the parlors after 1879.

Above: A corner of the back parlor.
Left: A paneled archway joins the two halves of the double parlor.

Page 137: Turn-of-the-century furniture, a Tiffany chandelier, and early-twentieth-century china, glassware, and tablecloth are used in the dining room.

Holley-Williams House

1807, Lakeville

The original house on this site was built before the Revolutionary War and was enlarged and transformed into an imposing Greek Revival edifice by John Milton Holley in 1807. Built on a mound above the road, the house and outbuildings exist today just as they were in the early nineteenth century; even the picket fence has been preserved. The dentil frieze decorating the pediment, the Corinthian capitals, and the doorway are all distinguished examples of Greek Revival architectural detail. Although Route 44 has replaced the country road, house and grounds still retain the dignity and quiet of a rural estate. At the time I was photographing the interior, deer from the woods behind the house were eating apples that had fallen from the trees in the garden.

The house was lived in by successive generations of the Holley family until it was bequeathed to the Salisbury Association in 1971 by Miss Margaret Holley Williams.

Above: Ball-fringed curtains in the parlor are draped in early-nineteenth-century style.
Left: A rear bedroom. The blue-and-white handwoven commemorative coverlet is reversible.

Page 141: Entrance hall. A rear door opens into the rose garden.

Left: An early illustration of the house.

Below: Recessed arches flank the parlor fireplace. One houses a spinet; the other frames the dining room door.

Aaron Bissel House

1812, Hartford County

This beautiful country house might well be known as the "bride's house," for through the years its new owners have been recently married couples. It was built in 1812 by Aaron Bissel for his daughter Sophia, who was married to Eli Bissel Haskell, her father's business partner, in 1810. The house remained in the family until 1931 when Joshua Coffin Chase bought the property with its guest house and extensive acres as a wedding gift for his daughter and son-in-law, Mr. and Mrs. Ralph C. Lasbury. Recently the house changed hands again; it was purchased by a young doctor and his bride. The photographs here show the house as it was while the Lasburys were still living there.

Mrs. Lasbury is a descendant of the famed New England heroine Hannah Dustin, who in 1697 was kidnapped by Indians from her home in Haverhill, Massachusetts, and taken with her newborn baby, the child's nurse, and a young boy to a place near what is now Concord, New Hampshire. Undaunted, Hannah tomahawked and scalped ten Indians and returned along the Merrimack River to her home. A painting portraying this dramatic event is seen in the photograph of the living room.

144

Above: The living room. The painting above the sofa depicts Hannah Dustin and her companions effecting their release from the Indians. *Right:* The front entrance.

146 Carved bird from Mr. Lasbury's extensive collection.

Left: A rear wing provides sheltered outdoor seating areas. Beyond it are a guest house and stables.

Above: Italian Renaissance furniture in the dining room reflects a period when Americans were adopting a more cosmopolitan way of life.

Page 145: The entrance hall.

Samuel Russell House

1827–1829, Middletown

In 1830, Samuel Russell, whose clipper ships were the fastest in the China trade, came home at last from Canton after nearly twenty years abroad. After a ninety-day journey in one of his own fast ships across the Pacific and around Cape Horn, he disembarked from his ship in the Connecticut River to see for the first time the Greek Revival façade of the house he had designed and had built for him while he was overseas. He had sent plans, specifications, and even a wooden model to his friend, Samuel D. Hubbard, with detailed instructions. In a letter to Hubbard written October 3, 1827, he specified ceiling heights, requested that the fireplaces be of marble (to cost about $60 each), and asked that the best door locks be brought from New York. He explained that he would order glass for the windows from Hamburg, Germany.

Correspondence with the New Haven architect Ithiel Town shows that he apparently was designated architect for the house; David Hoadley has been recorded as the builder. Russell's first estimate of the cost of the house and land was about $7500, but his wife, for whom it was built, set aside his original plans and the house cost about $12,-000 by the time it was finished. Less extravagantly, the impressive Corinthian columns, made for a New Haven bank that failed, were rescued by Hubbard and brought to the site by oxcart. The house was furnished with great elegance; its accoutrements included many superb pieces of Chinese furniture, china, and silks. When the orator-statesman Edward Everett (1794–1865) stayed with the Russells in 1859, he wrote of the house as "Russell Palace," saying, "Nothing could exceed the luxury of my quarters."

In 1860, Russell had the twenty-two-room mansion enlarged by the addition of a north wing to serve as a home for his orphaned grandson, Samuel Wadsworth Russell, who was born in 1847, and the east porch divided into three rooms. These alterations brought the number of rooms in the already capacious house to forty-two.

The house was occupied by the Russell family until 1936, when T. Macdonough Russell Jr. presented it to Wesleyan University.

Above : The entrance hall.
Above right: The front parlor. The painted designs on the ceiling, the cornice frieze, and the wall panels are as they were in 1830, although the furnishings of the room have been changed.
Right: The former back parlor.
Opposite page: A loggia overlooking a garden maze was once the dining room.

150

Alsop House

1836–1838, Middletown

Alsop House and Samuel Russell House are near neighbors on High Street in Middletown; when Charles Dickens visited the town on a lecture tour, he declared that this was the finest street in America.

Samuel Russell, who had received on-the-spot help for the building of his own house, in turn was able to oversee the building of this nearby house while his friend Richard Alsop IV continued his business trading with Chile and the West Indies from Philadelphia. By the time the work was done, Alsop's splendid mansion with its *trompe l'oeil* sculpture niches and painted decorations cost almost double the initially specified sum of $10,000; the final tally was $19,345.87.

Although the architect is not known, for a long time it was believed to be Ithiel Town (1784–1844), architect of Samuel Russell House. Town had an extensive architectural library and his works often were inspired by European sources. The exterior of Alsop House closely resembles a house in Potsdam, Germany, designed by Ludwig Persius. Many of the painted decorations on the interior walls are similar to those in Karl Friedrich Schinkel's Royal Palace in Potsdam. Some of the figures on the walls of Alsop House and two of the ceiling paintings of subjects from Greek mythology, "Apollo's Chariot" and "The Car of Jupiter," show the influence of Raphael.

The Greek Revival inspiration of Samuel Russell House is also present here in the columned wings, but the central portion of the façade has an Italianate air, an early example of this style in America. In 1829, Ithiel Town had taken into partnership Alexander Jackson Davis (1803–1892), who is credited with introducing the Italian Villa style to this country. Town and Davis were responsible for a great many Greek Revival public buildings, including the now-vanished Connecticut State Capitol in New Haven and the Customs House in New York. Alsop House represents a graceful blending of influences closely associated with Town, but recent research indicates that other architects may have been involved.

Wesleyan University purchased the house in 1949 for use as its Davison Art Center, appropriately furnished the front rooms with antiques of the Greek Revival period, and added a print gallery. Other rooms in the building are now used for workshops, classrooms, and exhibitions.

The stair hall.

Above : Painted flowers, ferns, and
vines decorate the morning room.
Above right: The dining room.

Above left: The back parlor.
Above: A mirror-backed pier table in the entrance hall.
Left: The front parlor.

Gothic Cottage

1840, Fairfield County

"The Cottage," as this thirty-five-room, eleven-staircase, thirteen-fireplace house has always been called, was designed in 1840 by the noted architect Joseph C. Wells as a summer house for Jonathan Sturges and his family. Sturges was an organizer and acting president and director of the Illinois Central Railroad, later a founder and president of the Union League Club in New York City, and founder and director of the Bank of Commerce in New York City.

Henry Fairfield, former president of the American Museum of Natural History, was born here; his mother was Virginia Reed Sturges. J. Pierpont Morgan, while courting his future bride, Amelia Sturges, carved his initials in the big beech tree on the back lawn; they are still visible in the bark.

Six generations of Sturges's descendants have lived in and still enjoy Gothic Cottage. Its furnishings include mementos of various periods harmoniously blended in a style that is essentially Victorian.

Above: The main entrance hall. A
print depicting George Washington's inaugural ball hangs over the
pier table.
Right: Amelia Sturges Morgan at
about the time of her marriage to J.
Pierpont Morgan.

Page 157: Another view of the hall.

Above left: In the dining room, a carved mahogany cupboard is built into the wall.
Left and above: Two views of the front parlor.

Lighthouse

1823 and 1841, Stonington

Stonington Lighthouse, the first established by the federal government in Connecticut, originally stood farther down along Stonington Point, but erosion around the base became so critical that in 1840 the tower was taken down and the granite blocks hauled to the present location on Water Street. The structure continued in service as a lighthouse until 1889, when a new lighthouse was built at Watch Hill, across Little Narragansett Bay. To guide mariners into Stonington Har-

bor, an oil-fueled lantern was installed on the town's west breakwater.

The octagonal stone tower was purchased by the Stonington Historical Society in 1910, and in 1925 it was opened as a museum. In addition to early stoneware, historic portraits, toys, tools, furniture, and Indian relics, the collection includes ship models, whaling gear, and Oriental curios, for Stonington, like most Connecticut coastal towns, has a long seafaring tradition.

Top: Portrait of Captain Charles Thompson Stanton of Stonington painted by Phineas Stanton c. 1850.
Above: Pitcher commemorating the Battle of Stonington.
Right: The former living quarters.

Page 161: Stoneware jugs and crocks are displayed on shelves.

Harriet Beecher Stowe House

1871, Hartford

In a little corner of Hartford known as Nook Farm, a small group of friends and relatives once shared a closely knit social and intellectual life. Two of Harriet Beecher Stowe's sisters, Isabella (Mrs. John Hooker) and Mary (Mrs. Thomas C. Perkins), and John Hooker's sister and brother-in-law, Elisabeth and Francis Gillette, already had their homes there when the author of *Uncle Tom's Cabin* and her husband, Calvin Stowe, came to join this congenial community in 1864.

There they built Mrs. Stowe's dream house, Oakholm, on the outskirts of the farm. When it proved financially burdensome, Oakholm was sold, and in 1873 the Stowes purchased the "cottage" pictured here. This new home was within a few steps of where

Mark Twain, a year later, built his nineteen-room mansion around the corner on Farmington Avenue.

Harriet Beecher Stowe (1811–1896) spent the last twenty years of her life here, although she wintered in Florida to escape Connecticut's cold.

The Stowe-Day Foundation, which owns and maintains the house, has restored it to look much as it did in the famous author's day. In the kitchen, they have incorporated many of the features of convenience and practicality advocated by *The American Woman's Home,* a practical and imaginative book of household management and interior decoration that she wrote with her oldest sister, Catherine E. Beecher.

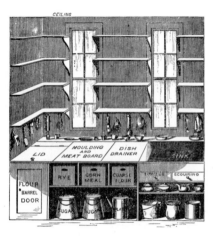
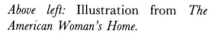

Above left: Illustration from *The American Woman's Home.*

Above right: The kitchen arrangements carry out Mrs. Stowe's ideas about convenience and efficiency. The open bin is designed to hold one hundred pounds of flour.

Right: Illustration from *The American Woman's Home.*

166

Above: The rear parlor. Mrs. Stowe had inherited many pieces of Beecher furniture, which she mixed with her own Victorian things.

Left: Harriet Beecher Stowe in the front parlor about 1886. (Photograph courtesy Stowe-Day Foundation.)

Page 165: The dining room.

Mark Twain House

1874, Hartford

This fanciful Victorian house at Nook Farm was designed for Mark Twain (1835–1910) by Edward Tuckerman Potter (1831–1904) and redecorated about six years later by Louis Comfort Tiffany's decorating firm, the Associated Artists. The geometric decorative stenciling covering the walls and ceilings was a hallmark of Tiffany style. Both in architecture and furnishings, the house appealed to Mark Twain's originality, his love of luxury, his sense of home. He spent some of his most fruitful, happy years here. Two of his children were born in this house; it was here he wrote *The Adventures of Tom Sawyer, The Adventures of Huckleberry Finn, A Connecticut Yankee in King Arthur's Court, A Tramp Abroad, The Prince and the Pauper,* and *Life on the Mississippi.*

After seventeen years in this house, financial difficulties forced him to take his family to Europe, where they could live less expensively and to go on a worldwide lecture tour to earn funds to pay his debts. In 1895, his favorite daughter Susy died and the family never returned to Nook Farm to live. In 1903, Mark Twain sold the house, but of his beloved home he wrote: "To us, our house was not unsentient matter—it had a heart, and a soul, and eyes to see us with; and approvals, and solicitudes, and deep sympathies; it was of us, and we were in its confidence, and lived in its grace and in the peace of its benediction. We never came home from an absence that its face did not light up and speak out its eloquent welcome—and we could not enter it unmoved." These words appear in a letter in the archives of the Mark Twain Memorial.

After the house was sold in 1903, it underwent drastic changes, but the Restoration Committee of the Mark Twain Memorial, and the former curator, Wilson H. Faude, have managed through extensive research to restore it to its earlier condition. Where necessary, such as in the dining room, wallpaper has been made and finished by hand to match the original, and the house once again glows with late Victorian warmth and splendor.

This is the house that Mark built.

These are the bricks of various hue
And shape and position, straight and
    askew,
With the nooks and angles and
    gables too,
Which make up the house presented
    to view,
The curious house that Mark built.

—Mark Twain in *Traveler's Record,*
January 1877,
Courtesy Mark Twain Memorial

Opposite: The front parlor or drawing room has salmon pink and silver stenciling, pastel blue velvet draperies, and light beige upholstery.

Above: In the dining room, the fireplace is flued so that a window could be placed above it. Hand-stenciled wallpaper resembles embossed leather.

Left: Mark Twain. (Photograph courtesy Mark Twain Memorial.)

Page 169: The hall decorated for Christmas. Tiffany stenciling decorates the walls and ceiling.

Hill-Stead

1899–1901, Farmington

After a visit to Hill-Stead, Henry James described it as the "Mount Vernon of Connecticut." With its pillared portico it does bear a resemblance to George Washington's eighteenth-century plantation house, but its furnishings reflect a much later fashion. The retirement home of Ohio iron magnate Alfred Atmore Pope, it was designed by the colorful architect Stanford White. Like many other nineteenth-century millionaires, Pope started his career with meager capital but soon accumulated a fortune sufficient to amass an important collection of paintings, prints, furniture, china, and *objets d'art.*

Pope's only child, Theodate, attended Miss Porter's School in Farmington. The beauty of the region so captivated her that she persuaded her parents to move to Connecticut, and there on a sloping site overlooking superb vistas of the Farmington River, Pope had Stanford White build Hill-Stead, carrying out ideas suggested by the owners.

Although Stanford White's firm of McKim, Mead and White designed many residences modeled after French chateaus, English country houses, and Italian villas for wealthy clients, Hill-Stead takes its inspiration from the traditional American Colonial mansion and blends happily with the prevailing architectural style of historic Farmington. In this instance, White evidently was more strongly influenced by his clients' taste and by ideas remembered from an 1877 sketching trip through New England coastal towns than he was by European sources.

Theodate Pope spent a good part of her life at Hill-Stead. In 1916, she married the distinguished American diplomat John Wallace Riddle, whom she met at a dinner party given by Anna Roosevelt Cowles (page 104). Mrs. Riddle and her husband had both traveled a great deal, and their friends came from many parts of the world. Among those they entertained at Hill-Stead were Henry James, Mary Cassatt, the Roosevelts, John Masefield, and Sir Wilfred Grenfell.

An architect of merit, Theodate Pope Riddle designed and built the English Cotswold-style buildings of Avon Old Farms School for Boys in nearby Avon, which she established and endowed. Mrs. Riddle died in 1946, leaving the house to become a museum that is a tribute to a special life style as well as the home of a splendid art collection.

172

Above: The morning room.

Above: Stanford White. (Photograph courtesy New-York Historical Society.)

174